The
Mediterranean
By **Leighton Taylor**
Sea

B L A C K B I R C H   P R E S S ,   I N C .

W O O D B R I D G E ,   C O N N E C T I C U T

TABLE OF CONTENTS

Published by Blackbirch Press, Inc.
260 Amity Road
Woodbridge, CT 06525

©1999 by Blackbirch Press, Inc.
First Edition

e-mail: staff@blackbirch.com
Web site: www.blackbirch.com

Text ©Leighton Taylor
Printed in the United States
10 9 8 7 6 5 4 3 2 1

Editor's Note

The photos that appear on pages 16–18, 26, and 42 show species that are found in the Mediterranean, but the photos were taken in a different locale. Because no suitable images of the species could be found in a Mediterranean environment, these very similar images were used instead.

Library of Congress Cataloging-in-Publication Data

Taylor, L.R. (Leighton R.)
The Mediterranean Ocean / by Leighton Taylor; featuring the photographs of Norbert Wu
     p.   cm. — (Life in the sea)
     Includes bibliographical references and index.
     ISBN 1-56711-247-1
     1. Mediterranean Sea—Juvenile literature. I. Wu, Norbert. II. Title. III. Series: Taylor, L.R. (Leighton R.) Life in the sea
GC651.T39   1999
551.46'2—dc21   98-42082
                                                                              CIP
                                                                               AC

IMAGINE A COOL, GREEN SEA

Imagine a large oval sea almost enclosed by land. Only a small channel with a shallow sill connects it to an ocean. The waters of this sea are sometimes green, sometimes blue, sometimes warm, sometimes cool. Along its rocky shores and on its sandy and muddy bottoms live thousands of animals and plants. Many were known to the people who lived on the shores of this sea more than 2,000 years ago.

B AN OCEAN "IN THE MIDDLE"

ut you don't have to imagine such a sea! The Mediterranean is such a place!

The name "Mediterranean" comes from ancient Latin words that mean "the middle of the earth." To the Greeks and Romans who thrived around this sea about 2,000 years ago, the Mediterranean was the middle of their known world. They did not know about the Pacific Ocean or the Caribbean Sea or many other parts of the earth.

The Mediterranean barely connects to the Atlantic Ocean by a narrow channel between Spain and North Africa called the Strait of Gibraltar. The Mediterranean also has a narrow connection to the much smaller dead-end Black Sea, which is surrounded by Russia, Turkey, Ukraine, and other countries.

The Mediterranean Sea washes the shores of Israel, Lebanon, Syria, and other countries of the Middle East. It also separates the subcontinent of Europe from Northern Africa.

The Mediterranean washes the shores of Europe, Africa, and parts of the Middle East.
Inset: **The rocky Mediterranean coastline of Majorca island, off the eastern coast of Spain.**

4

THE NATURE OF THE OCEAN

When astronauts look at Earth from space, they see a planet mostly covered by water. Some people call our Earth "Planet Ocean." That's because it has much more ocean than dry land.

From space, the world's ocean looks the same all over. But it can be very different from place to place. The water can be different. The location and shape of the holes filled by seawater can be special.

How is seawater different from one place to another? Here are three important ways that seawater can change, depending on:

1. how warm or cold it is
2. how much salt it holds
3. how clear or murky it is

The surface seawater in the Mediterranean Sea gets very warm in the summer. Water evaporates into clouds. The seawater left behind is very salty and heavy. It sinks deeper. Cooler water from the Atlantic Ocean flows in the Strait of Gibraltar to take its place.

Oceanographers are scientists who study the ocean. They can tell a lot about the currents in the Mediterranean Sea by using satellites. Cameras and instruments on satellites record the temperature, movement, and level of the ocean currents on the surface of the sea. Oceanographers also use ships to take water temperatures and measure ocean saltiness below the surface.

All this information helps them do many things—study currents and the winds, predict weather, help fishermen find fish, help sea captains save fuel, and a lot more.

The rock of Gibraltar soars high above the Mediterranean on Spain's southern coast.

MORE THAN SEVEN SEAS—THE MANY WATERS OF THE WORLD

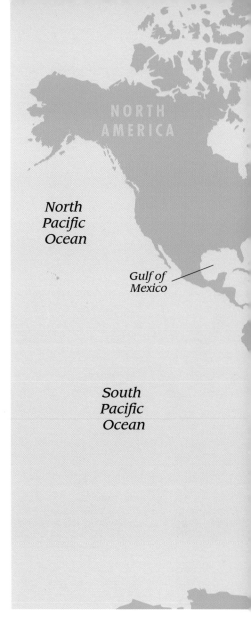

NORTH AMERICA

North Pacific Ocean

Gulf of Mexico

South Pacific Ocean

The location and shape of a basin filled by seawater gives each body of water special characteristics. The earth's seawater fits into holes of many different sizes and shapes. These giant holes are shaped by the land around them. The names for these different areas of seawater depend on their size and shape.

An *ocean* is the biggest area of seawater. An ocean is so big, it touches several continents. It can take many days to cross an ocean, even in a fast boat. The Pacific Ocean is the world's largest ocean. The Atlantic Ocean and the Indian Ocean are very large, too.

A *sea* is smaller than an ocean but still very big. A sea is more enclosed by land than an ocean and may touch only a few countries or even be in the middle of a single country. Sailing the "Seven Seas" is an old sailor's term. In reality, there are many more seas than seven. The Mediterranean Sea is a big, famous sea. It is connected to the Red Sea by the Suez Canal. The Caribbean Sea touches Florida and Mexico and has many islands.

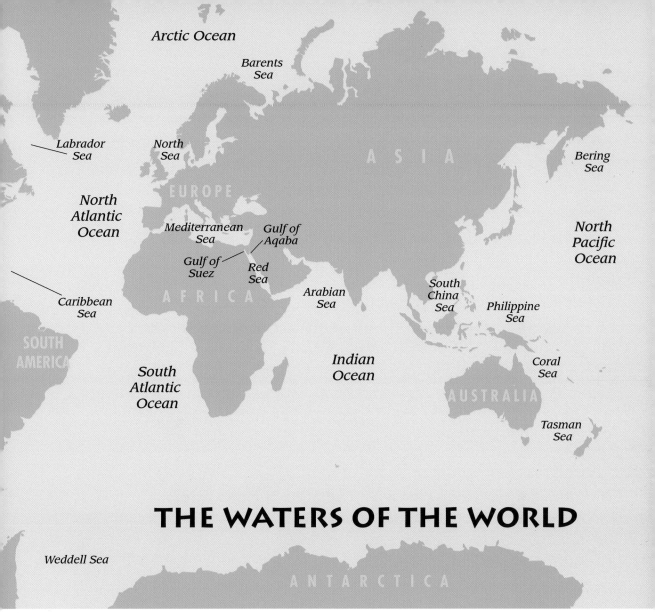

THE WATERS OF THE WORLD

Smaller parts of the ocean can be called a *gulf*. Sometimes gulfs are big, sometimes small. The Gulf of Mexico is very big. The Gulf of Aqaba (AH-ka-ba) and the Gulf of Suez are small. These gulfs are at the very top of the Red Sea.

EXPLORING THE MEDITERRANEAN SEA

You can experience thrills exploring the Mediterranean Sea, both on and under the surface. Begin your exploration in a good research ship. It could be similar to the *Calypso*, which the famous captain Jacques Cousteau used to explore this sea.

First, enter from the Atlantic Ocean and head east. This will send you through the Strait of Gibraltar, which is the waterway that lies between the northernmost tip of Africa and the southernmost tip of Europe. It is only eight miles wide. On your right is Morocco and the continent of Africa. On your left is Spain, part of Europe.

About 1,200 miles out into the ocean, stop and snorkel or scuba dive along the coast of the island of Sicily. On a map, Sicily looks like a lumpy football being kicked by the boot of Italy. The water here, as in most of the Mediterranean Sea, is not cold. But, it is not as warm as the water in the Caribbean Sea, the tropical Pacific Ocean, or the Red Sea.

A curious grouper swims past a diver who sits in a rocky reef.

_➤ **The Mediterranean monk seal is the world's rarest seal.**

As you dive beneath the surface into clear water you will see rocky reefs (the Mediterranean has no coral reefs). The fishes—wrasses, damselfish, groupers, jacks—look a lot like their relatives in the Caribbean and the warm Pacific Ocean, but they are different species. More than 12,000 kinds of sea animals and plants live in the Mediterranean. About 4,000 of them live nowhere else.

After you finish your scuba dive, sail further east toward Greece.

If you are really lucky, you might get a glimpse of the rarest seal in the world, the Mediterranean monk seal. These seals are almost extinct. Unfortunately, European fishermen are still killing them so their boats can haul in more fish.

Wherever you go on the Mediterranean, you'll be sailing in waters that have been at the center of some of the richest history on earth. Because humans have lived near and on this special sea for thousands of years, these waters have witnessed the birth and death of some of our greatest civilizations.

RED CORAL TREASURE

Precious red coral grows in caves and underneath overhanging rocks deep in the Mediterranean Sea. Red coral is only distantly related to the reef-building corals of the tropical Indian Ocean, Pacific Ocean, and Caribbean Sea. Red corals are more closely related to the sea fans of tropical reefs. Red corals have hard skeletons of beautiful colors including rose, scarlet, and crimson.

After the soft animals that made the red skeletons are dried and scrubbed off, jewelers can polish the red branches and carve them. Red coral jewelry and sculptures have been highly valued by many people for thousands of years. Ancient Greek and Roman artists polished and carved priceless statues of coral. Five hundred years ago Italian artists painted grand pictures of Jesus and Mary wearing red coral bracelets, necklaces and rings.

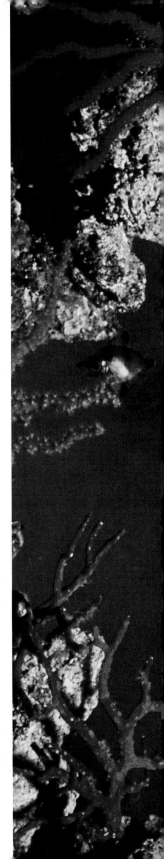

Left: **Polished red coral pieces serve as the raw materials for jewelry.**
Opposite: **A garden of red coral grows amid a rocky enclave.**
Inset: **A beautiful red coral necklace.**

 A hair-like byssus glues mussels to solid surfaces and holds them secure.

FEEL THESE MUSSELS

Some rocky shores of the Mediterranean have large colonies of purple-black mussels. These mollusks are relatives of clams and cockles that live in the mud and sand. Mussels, however, prefer to live in surf-swept rocks and moving water.

With all the pounding surf, how do mussels keep from being washed away? Living close together and forming a rough cover for the rocks helps cushion the force of waves. But a mussel's real secret for holding on looks like a stringy brown beard. Each mussel has a gland that makes many strong hairs called a byssus (BIS-SUS). These threads glue onto the rocks and hold the mussel securely.

Many people love to eat the soft flesh of mussels, but what do mussels eat? They certainly can't hunt while they are glued to a rock! The waves bring their food to them. Very tiny plants and animals swimming in sea water are sucked into the mussel.

Sometimes mussels filter out chemicals and bacteria from polluted water. When they do this, they can eat tiny poisonous creatures. None of this hurts the mussel much. But people who eat bacteria-filled mussels can get very sick or, in some cases, can even die.

◄ **A large colony of purple mussels clings together.**

PADDLE WORMS AND FIRE WORMS

Imagine a creature whose long strong body is made up of a string of repeating parts—like a bead bracelet. It has four eyes and strong jaws that contain zinc and copper. Four pairs of long tentacles wriggle ahead of it as it creeps along, hunting for a victim. Its sides are covered with poisonous bristles and strong fin-like paddles. For its size, it is one of the most vicious predators in the ocean.

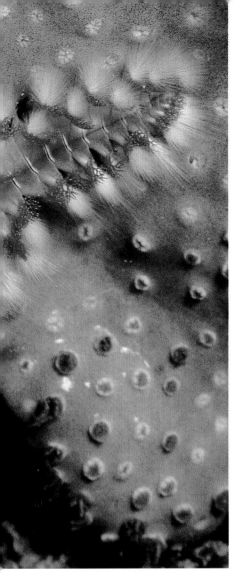

These wormy hunters of the Mediterranean are called polychaetes (POLLY-KEETS). The name comes from Greek words meaning "many hairs," which are actually the poisonous bristles on their sides. Most polychaetes are about as long as your hand. Some Mediterranean polychaetes have very strong poison. Touching them can cause a painful burn.

Polychaetes are relatives of the earthworms and night crawlers you find in your backyard and garden. These worms eat dirt and do not have any spines or bristles.

Fireworms (above) and paddleworms (right) are some of the Mediterranean's most dangerous and poisonous predators.

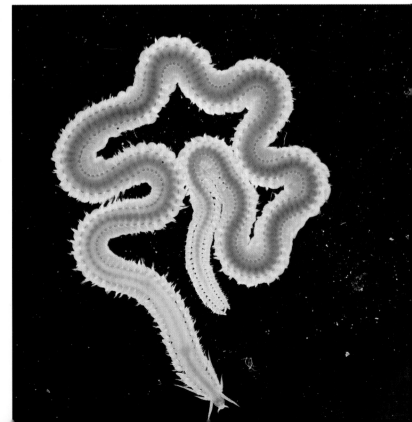

FISH THAT FLY

Birds can swim but can fish fly? Some can—or at least they can glide through the air. Several kinds of flying fish live in the open surface waters of the Mediterranean Sea. When chased by bigger hunting fish such as tuna, sharks, and swordfish, a flying fish makes strong rapid strokes with its big tail. When it breaks through the surface of the sea, it soars with the wind and appears to fly. It can glide for hundreds of feet using its long, broad "arm fins" or pectoral fins as wings. The fish chasing a flying fish loses sight of it and cannot see where the flying fish dives back into the water.

Some flying fish species have four distinct wings.
Inset: **The mottled skin of this flying gurnard matches the surroundings on the ocean bottom.**

Most fishes have tails that are the same size on the top and the bottom. Flying fish have a much larger bottom part of their tail fins. The tail helps the fish in two ways. Its strong fin drives the fish forward and up. It can also be dragged along the water's surface to steer the fish during flight.

Other fish in the Mediterranean Sea, unrelated to flying fish, also have very big pectoral fins. Despite its name, the flying gurnard never leaves the water. It spreads its large spotted "wings" to look much larger and less like a good meal for a hunting fish.

STARGAZERS

On the bottom of the Mediterranean Sea, in shallow water, pairs of eyes look toward the sky. The eyes belong to a strange kind of fish about as long as your forearm. Called "stargazers," these big-mouthed, well-camouflaged fish hide in the sand, waiting for an unsuspecting shrimp or fish to swim by. When they do, they will become a stargazer's meal.

Stargazers can attract small animals to their hiding places by wiggling the small, worm-like flaps on their lower lip. Even the scientific name of the stargazer reflects its upward-looking eyes. *Uranoscopus* means "looking at Uranus," a faraway planet (not a star!).

Behind a stargazer's eyes, in the muscles on the top of its head, are some special organs. The tissues in these highly adapted muscles can produce electric shocks. Stargazers may use these electric generators to stun prey, or frighten away predators. A person or fish who catches a stargazer can get an unpleasant shock by just touching the fish's head.

Flat-bodied stargazers are masters of camouflage.

🐟 A parasitic arthropod clings to the body of a silverfish.

DO FISH HAVE FLEAS?

Do fish have fleas? No, but relatives of fleas sometimes live on fish. These "fish fleas" are more closely related to shrimp and crabs. They are usually big compared to the fish. A fish as big as your hand may have a "fish flea" bigger than a large postage stamp. Usually only one "fish flea" hangs on to one fish at a time.

The tiny black fleas on dogs and cats are insects, like flies, beetles, and mosquitoes. But they are all related to the "fish fleas," and to crabs, lobsters, and shrimp. All these animals share enough common features—like jointed legs—that scientists consider them related to each other. The very big group that they all belong to is called the arthropods (AHR-THROW-PODS). "Arthro" means jointed, and "pod" means foot or leg. So it's true that cats, dogs, and fish all get arthropods on them sometimes!

THE CAVE BENEATH THE SEA

≈≈≈≈≈≈≈≈≈≈≈≈≈≈≈≈≈≈≈≈≈

Imagine you are standing in a damp, dark cave of limestone inside a white cliff on the coast of France. There is no way to get here and stay dry. You must wear scuba gear, dive down to 120 feet (37 meters), and swim and crawl almost 500 feet (152 meters) upwards through a narrow, dark passageway. When you come to the sea surface, you are in a dark cave, like a large room with a rocky shelf to climb out on.

Shine your waterproof flashlight on the walls and ceiling.

The walls are covered with ancient paintings! Scientists and explorers have found paintings of auks, seals, fish, human handprints, and something that looks a lot like jellyfish medusas. They have also analyzed some of the red and black colors to test the age of the paintings. A few painted hand prints are 27,000 years old—the oldest human cave paintings ever found!

But how did the ancient artists enter the cave? They climbed and walked through the same narrow passageway that today's scuba divers use—but 27,000 years ago the level of the Mediterranean Sea was about 350 feet (107 meters) lower than it is now. Long ago, much of the water from the ocean was frozen in glaciers in the northern part of the earth. Scientists call that time the Ice Age. As the glaciers melted, the sea level gradually got higher. Sea level 100 years in the future will be more than 3 feet (1 meter) higher than it is now.

SNAIL TALES

Many kinds of sea slugs and sea snails live in the Mediterranean. Some are smaller than the fingernail on your pinky. Others are large enough to cover your entire hand. Some are colorful and some are drab. A few of the dullest-looking snails can be used to make some very colorful dyes. The murex snail, for example, was used to make dye thousands of years ago.

Tyrian royal purple dye was a valuable reddish-violet dye used to make clothing for wealthy Roman nobles. The dye chemical is made by glands near the sea snail's anus. When it mixes with air it changes into green, yellow, blue and then crimson.

A murex snail finds cover in some tall sea grass.

◄ **Nudibranchs show us their colors while they are alive. Their drab-shelled relatives provide color for dyes after they die.**

An early center of dye making was the ancient city of Tyre (now just ruins in the modern country of Lebanon). The dye has long been called Tyrian purple. Tyrian dye-makers crushed the whole snail to get the chemical. The dye was very valuable. About 10,000 snails were crushed to make just 1 gram of dye! Lebanon has big piles of shells left by dye-makers who worked almost 2,000 years ago.

A close-up view of a sea cucumber's mouth.

UNWANTED PEARLS

One of the strangest fish in the Mediterranean Sea is the pearlfish. It is about as long as your little finger but even smaller around. Pearlfish live inside the guts of sea cucumbers. Sometimes they come out and look around and then quickly squirm back inside through the sea cucumber's anus.

Inside the gut of the sea cucumber, the pearlfish is safe. But this relationship is a bad deal for the sea cucumber. The pearlfish actually eats the sex organs of its host. Sometimes the sea cucumber tries to get rid of its unwanted guest. It forces its guts inside out and pushes the pearlfish into the open water.

How did such a weird fish get such a pretty name? Sometimes pearlfish live inside big pearl oysters. When the fish dies inside the oyster, the oyster's shell forms a shiny covering over it, making a pearl from the fish.

Top: **A pearlfish peeks out from inside a sea cucumber's body.**
Middle: **The pearlfish emerges from the rear of its host.**
Bottom: **Fully exposed, the pearlfish shows it is nearly as long as the sea cucumber it inhabits!**

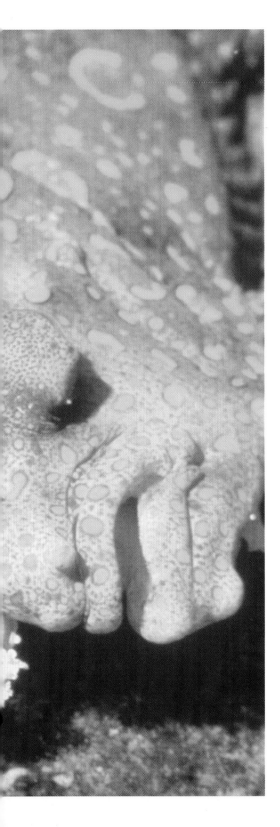

THINGS ARE LOOKING UP

Many fish that are good hiders will rest on a sandy or muddy bottom area. Such fish hide for two reasons—to avoid being eaten by bigger fish, and to ambush smaller animals they want to eat. To hide and to hunt requires camouflage and good eyesight. Many hiding fish are able to change the colors and patterns of their skin so they blend into their surroundings.

It also helps to stay low. The flatter a hiding fish is, the harder it is to see on a bottom surface. And a really big advantage for a bottom-hiding, hunting fish would be to be very flat, but have a big mouth, and two big eyes. It would also help if a fish were thin and had both eyes on one side of its head! Well, flatfish, halibuts, and soles all have both eyes on the same side of their bodies. That's why they're such successful predators. They can lay flat on the ocean bottom and look straight up to see danger or food.

Two eyes on one side of its head—and mottled skin that camouflages perfectly—make the Mediterranean sole a stealthy hunter and an expert hider.

JELLIES THAT HUNT AND KILL

When we think of hunters in the Mediterranean Sea, we most often think of sharks, tuna, or dolphins. Few people, however, think about jellyfish and their relative—the Portuguese man-of-war—as hunters. These creatures, however, can be some of the ocean's most deadly predators.

Jellyfish and their relatives belong to a large group of animals that scientists call the Cnidaria. All the animals in this group have circular, jelly-like bodies, a big central mouth, and stinging cells filled with tiny poisonous arrows.

These stinging cells are the reason for the name Cnidaria. The name is based on an ancient Greek word for "nettle." Nettle is a common plant in Europe and America. When you touch a nettle leaf you get a painful rash. If you touch the stinging cells of a Cnidaria animal, it can hurt, too. Cnidaria use their stinging cells for protection and for feeding. Each tiny stinging cell contains a long coiled thread with a sharp, poisonous point. When a small shrimp, or fish—or swimmer's leg—brushes against the stinging cell, it fires. The cell bursts open, the thread uncoils, and the sharp point injects poison. Usually, many cells fire together. Their combined poison and tangled threads make Cnidaria good hunters. They can also make them painful to run into.

A swarm of jellyfish sways in the Mediterranean current.

The Portuguese man-of-war is a familiar "jellyfish" to beach-goers in the western Mediterranean. Their long purple tentacles have very strong stinging cells. These cells can sting even after the man-of-war has drifted onto the beach. Portuguese man-of-wars float on the sea surface. Their gas-filled float is blown by the wind. Because they sail and are well-armed, they are named after a kind of old sailing ship. Four hundred years ago, ships from Portugal began to explore the world. The biggest ships carried many cannons. Such a ship was called a "man-of-war."

The Portuguese man-of-war belongs to the Cnidaria. But, they are not like other jellyfish, called "medusas." A medusa is one individual animal. But a Portuguese man-of-war is actually a colony of related individuals. It is a group of many animals that are connected. Beneath the float are clusters of medusas and polyps.

The Portuguese man-of-war has long purple tentacles and powerful stinging cells.

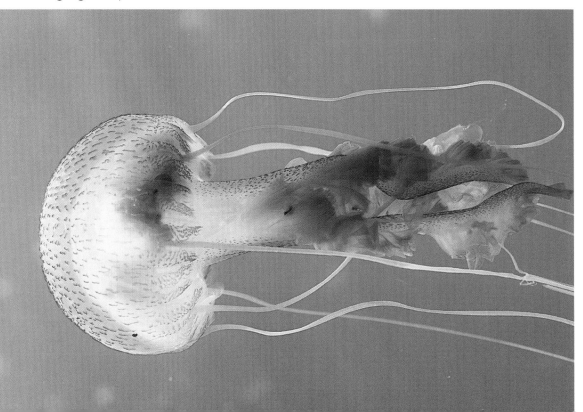

A SEA OF GODS AND GODDESSES
≈≈≈≈≈≈≈≈≈≈≈≈≈≈≈≈≈≈≈≈

Almost totally surrounded by land, the Mediterranean has the longest recorded human history of all the world's seas. Twenty thousand years ago the people who lived in Southern France painted pictures on the walls of seaside caves. Three thousand years ago, the Egyptians, Greeks, and Romans believed the storms, waves, and sea creatures were part of another world that was controlled by many gods and goddesses who lived there.

The gods and beasts of the Mediterranean Sea were especially important to the Greeks. One of the most important Greek gods was Okeanos. He was the son of Uranus (Heaven) and Gaea (Earth). We get the word "ocean" from his name. The Greeks believed that Okeanos was the father of 3,000 ocean nymphs—or sea spirits.

One of these daughters was named Amphitrite (AM-FY-TRY-TEE). Poseidon, the Greek god of the sea, fell in love with Amphitrite when he saw her dance. There is a graceful sea worm that lives in the Mediterranean; it reminded modern scientists of her legendary beauty, so they named the worm after her.

Not all the ocean personalities in Greek legends were beautiful. The great monster Scylla lived in a grim seaside cave, ambushed sailors, and ate dolphins. Some scientists think that Scylla may have been a giant squid that once scared the stuffing out of Greek sailors!

ONE THOUSAND YEARS OF SPONGES

There are more than 5,000 kinds of sponges in the world's waters. Some sponges live in warm shallow seas such as the Mediterranean Sea. Others live in the very deep and icy waters of the Arctic and Antarctic.

There are sponges in the Mediterranean that humans have used for thousands of years. Paintings of ancient Greek urns show people using sponges to bathe. The Greeks also used them to scrub floors and to pad war helmets and armor. The Romans used sponges as paint brushes and as mops, as well as to scrub themselves when they washed. Greeks and Romans burned sponges in their homes so the smoke would kill bugs.

Thousands of small pockets make up the surface of a sponge. *Insets*: A coral sponge (left) and a rock covered with multi-colored sponges (below).

How did the Greeks and Romans get all the sponges they used? Swimmers held their breath, dove down to the bottom, and ripped the sponges from rocks. To humans, the most useful part of a sponge is the skeleton. Living sponges are dried and rinsed so only the spongy skeleton remains. When a sponge is alive the many, many tiny holes in its body filter sea water for food. These same holes in a dead, dry sponge skeleton can soak up bath water, paint, wine, or any liquid. Some people still use real sponges, but most "sponges" today are produced in factories from plastics and other materials.

Many colorful kinds of sponges grow on the Mediterranean's underwater rocks.
***Inset top:* A diver explores the sponge garden that has developed on a sunken B17 U.S. warplane.**
***Inset bottom:* Greek stores in the old market section of Athens sell sponges of all kinds.**

BIRTHPLACE OF SCUBA

We know a lot more about ocean life now than we did 50 years ago. One reason for this is the development of scuba gear. The best way to learn about creatures in the sea is to watch them up close. People have tried to do this for thousands of years. But, it's hard for humans to get along underwater. We can't breathe like fish can. We can't hold our breath for a long time like dolphins can. Our naked eyes cannot focus—everything looks blurry.

People solved the vision problem first. With air in front of our eyes, we can focus them and see clearly. Goggles, face masks, and brass helmets help us to see underwater. But how can we breathe there? At first, people tried to cover their heads with a waterproof helmet. A helper pumped air into a hose connected to the helmet and the diver breathed it. This worked fairly well but it was hard to move around freely underwater.

Scuba is a self-contained system that allows people of all skills and ages to explore underwater worlds.

◀ **Advances in scuba equipment have enabled divers (and scientists) to explore the seas in great detail.** *Inset:* **Jacques Cousteau**

In 1943, working in the waters of the Mediterranean Sea off the coast of France, two men advanced diving into the twentieth century. An invention, made by oceanographer Jacques Cousteau and Emile Gagnen, revolutionized underwater exploration. It was called scuba and it has helped millions of people since to see beneath the sea. Scientists, fish-watchers, photographers—even children—can use scuba to breathe underwater.

Scuba is the name for the steel tank of compressed air and the hoses and valves that a diver uses to breathe air. *Scuba* is now a word. But for many years it was spelled "S.C.U.B.A." The letters stood for Self Contained Underwater Breathing Apparatus.

The great variety of sea life in the Mediterranean has provided food for people for centuries. But, overfishing has nearly wiped out fish, mussels, and other creatures in many areas of the Mediterranean. Today, strict rules about fishing help to protect endangered species.

Despite a dwindling mix of species, European markets are filled with many kinds of fishes. One of the most famous and popular Mediterranean seafood dishes is Bouillabaisse (BOOL-YA-BASE), which is a classic fish stew. The list of fish ingredients for bouillabaisse looks like the program for a Mediterranean-theme aquarium. Many "purists" say a good bouillabaisse includes only fish varieties found in the Mediterranen: John Dory, monkfish, bream, red mullet, whiting, sea bass, conger eel, red gurnard, and rascasse (a scorpion fish).

Red mullet

Clockwise from left: John Dory, scorpion fish, monkfish, conger eel

A SEA OF CHANGE

Imagine you are a Greek sponge diver living 500 years ago. You take a deep breath, dive from your small boat, and swim to the bottom to grab a sponge. The water is clear and clean and filled with fish. The bottom is richly covered with sponges and seaweeds. Crabs and shrimp scurry between rocks. A shadow from a huge school of tuna passes across the bottom.

A pod of bottlenose dolphins cruises through the ocean water.

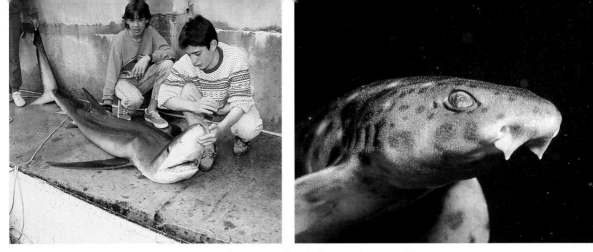

Left: **A blue shark that has been pulled from the Mediterranean.**
Right: **A chain cat shark, a small species common to the Mediterranean.**

Now, imagine you are there today. You dive from the boat. The water is sort of clear. Only a few fish swim by. There are no shadows from tuna. What happened?

One hundred thirty million people live on the shores of the Mediterranean Sea. For years, they have been careless with this fragile habitat. They have dumped trash, sewage, and chemicals into it. They have taken too many fish out of it. In some places, the sea is almost dead. Few fish live there and some are filled with chemicals that poison the animals that eat them.

The sea has changed from healthy to sick. But there is hope it will become healthy again. As long as 40 years ago, people who love the Mediterranean, like Captain Jacques Cousteau, warned the world to be more careful about polluting our seas. He and other naturalists devoted much of their lives to promoting a new understanding and respect for the world's oceans. Cousteau alone raised millions of dollars for research and conservation efforts.

Today, the countries around the Mediterranean, along with the United Nations, are trying to clean up the sea and to stop overfishing. Their efforts, and the continued education of people that use the sea, make it possible that someday the Mediterranean will be healthy and rich with life again.

HOW DO YOU MAP AN OCEAN?

A taxi driver can find an address by using a map and street signs. But how can a sailor find a location on the broad, empty ocean? When a boat sails near land, sailors can recognize landmarks. A map, or even a drawing of mountains and cliffs and beaches, can help them find their way. Some of the first maps made by sailors were made on the Red Sea. We know that the Egyptian Queen Hatshepsut sailed the length of the Red Sea about 2,500 years ago.

But in the open sea, away from land, there aren't any signs. And how can you make a map of a place that is all ocean?

Here's how: All mapmakers have agreed on two kinds of imaginary lines that cover the earth. One set of lines go from the top of the earth—at the North Pole—to the bottom of the earth—at the South Pole. These are the lines of "longitude" (lonj-EH-tood). The other lines that go around the earth from east to west are lines of "latitude" (lat-EH-tood). The latitude line that goes around the fattest part of the earth (at its middle) is called the equator. Above the equator is the Northern half of the earth, also known as the Northern Hemisphere. Below the equator is the Southern part of the earth. That's the Southern Hemisphere.

The equator is easy to find on a globe. But mapmakers also divide the earth in half going north to south. This line divides the world into two halves, too—the western half and the eastern half. Every line is numbered with degrees as they move around the circular earth.

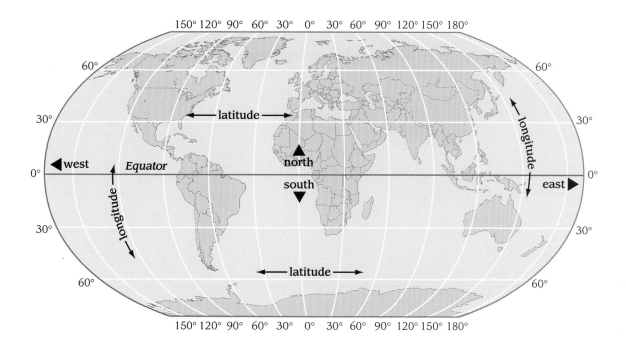

You can find places in the Mediterranean Sea on a map of the world by using "positions." A position is the place where a particular place on the latitude and a particular place on the longitude meet.

To find the Mediterranean at the Strait of Gibraltar, first find the longitude line for 10 degrees west. Find the latitude line for 38 degrees north. The two lines will cross in the Strait of Gibraltar.

But such lines only appear on maps. Nobody can actually draw them on the ocean! So how do sailors find their positions? By looking at the sky! At any given time, the moon, stars, and the sun are in predictable places. If a navigator knows what time it is and can measure the location of the sun, moon, or a few stars, he or she can find a position on Earth.

A new and even easier way has recently been invented. Navigators can use small computers that use satellites instead of stars to find a position of latitude and longitude.

GLOSSARY

camouflage To hide by looking like what's around you.

current A small or large body of water that is moving slower or faster than the water around it.

Equator The imaginary line of latitude that goes around the waist of the Earth (from east to west).

gulf A large part of an ocean or sea that reaches into the land.

latitude Imaginary lines that go around the earth from east to west (side to side). Map makers draw them on maps to show where places are located.

longitude Imaginary lines that go around the earth from north to south (up to down). Map makers draw them on maps to show where places are located.

navigation Finding where you are (your **position**) by using mathematics, time, stars, and maps.

oceanographer A scientist who studies the ocean and seas—including their currents, waves, plants and animals.

position The exact place where someone or something is, described as a point where a specific latitude and specific longitude meet.

salinity The amount of chemicals dissolved in seawater. The salinity of pure water is zero; the salinity of seawater is more than 3%.

FOR MORE INFORMATION

Books

Ackerman, Diane, Bill Curtsinger. *Monk Seal Hideaway.* New York, NY: Crown Publishing Group, 1995.

Italia, Bob. *Scuba Diving* (Action Sports Library). Minneapolis, MN: Abdo & Daughters, 1994.

Lambert, David. *The Mediterranean Sea* (Seas and Oceans). Chatham, NJ: Raintree/Steck-Vaughn, 1997.

Markham, Lois. *Jacques-Yves Cousteau: Exploring the Wonders of the Deep* (Innovative Minds). Chatham, NJ: Raintree/Steck-Vaughn, 1997.

Parker, Jane. *Seas & Oceans* (Take Five Geography). Danbury, CT: Franklin Watts, Inc., 1998.

Phillips, Anne W. *The Ocean* (Earth Alert). Glendale, CA: Crestwood House, 1990.

Rodgers, Mary M., Mary K. Hoff. *Oceans* (Our Endangered Planet). Minneapolis, MN: Lerner Publications Co., 1992.

Savage, Stephen. *Animals of the Ocean* (Animals by Habitat series). Chatham, NJ: Raintree/Steck-Vaughn, 1997.

Tesar, Jenny. *What on Earth is a Nudibranch?* (What on Earth? series). Woodbridge, CT: Blackbirch Press, Inc., 1995.

Web Site

Cetacea
A great page for dolphin and whale information—
www.geocities.com/RainForest/canopy/1599

INDEX

Photo credits

Page 3: ©PhotoDisc; pages 4–5: ©Daniel Bay; page 5 (inset): ©J.C. Carton/Bruce Coleman, Inc.; page 10: ©Daniel Bay; page 11: ©C. Pergent; page 12: ©Robert Pelham/Bruce Coleman, Inc.; pages 12–13: ©Yves Berard/Musee Oceanographique Monaco; page 13 (inset): ©Musee Oceanographique Monaco; page 14: ©Daniel Bay; page 15: ©Patrick Louisy; pages 16–17: ©Larry Lipsky/Bruce Coleman, Inc.; page 17: ©Bruce Coleman, Inc.; pages 18–19: ©Jane Burton/Bruce Coleman, Inc.; page 19 (inset): ©Patrick Louisy; pages 20–21: ©Daniel Bay; page 22: ©Daniel Bay; page 24: ©Daniel Bay; page 25: ©Daniel Bay; page 26: ©Bill Wood/Bruce Coleman, Inc.; page 27: ©Daniel Bay; pages 28–29: ©Daniel Bay; pages 30–31: ©Daniel Bay; page 32: ©Daniel Bay; page 33: ©Northwind Picture Archives; pages 34–35: ©Daniel Bay; page 35 (insets): ©Daniel Bay; pages 36–37: ©Daniel Bay; page 37 (top inset): ©Daniel Bay; page 37 (bottom inset): ©Diana Gleasner/Viesti Associates, Inc.; page 38: ©Daniel Bay; page 39: ©Daniel Bay; page 39 (inset): ©P. Martin–Razi; page 40: ©Daniel Bay; page 41: ©Daniel Bay, except bottom right: ©Musée Oceanographique de Monaco; page 42: ©Tui De Roy/Bruce Coleman, Inc.; page 43 (insets): ©Daniel Bay; page 44: ©Norbert Wu.